Frugal Living

The Definitive Money Management Handbook to Building Wealth and Achieving Financial Freedom

Jocelyn Lee

All Rights Reserved. No part of this publication may be reproduced in any form or by any means, including scanning, photocopying, or otherwise without prior written permission of the copyright holder. Copyright © 2014

Table of Contents

Introduction

Chapter 1

   What is frugal living?

      Frugal living means wise money management

      Frugal living means smart spending

      Frugal living means being creative

Chapter 2

   Why live frugally?

Chapter3

   How to break your bad spending habits

      Use cash always

      Making a shopping list always

      Have some 'spend-nothing' days

      Maintain a spending log

      Avoid certain websites and stores

Chapter 4

   How to develop a good monthly spending plan

      Total your earnings

      Make an assessment of your monthly expenses

- Get the difference between your earnings and monthly expenses
- Subtract other extra expenses
- Create a cushion
- Rework your budget
- Invest in yourself

Chapter 5

Putting your spending plan to work

Chapter 6

How to eliminate your personal debt
- Use common sense
- Avoid impulse buying
- Develop a good plan
- Research on various options that will help you save money
- Take action

Chapter 7

Psychology of frugal living: are you ready?

Chapter 8

Emergency fund and its importance
- Decide the amount of money you would like to save
- Determine your monthly expenses
- Open an account
- Know how much money you can save comfortably

- Setting up automatic deposits will help a lot
- Find alternative ways of boosting your savings
- 10 reasons you should have an emergency fund

Chapter 9

Tips on how to adapt to a frugal lifestyle

Chapter 10

Frugal living ideas for happy retirement

Chapter 11

7 important frugal habits you should develop
- Be proactive
- Focus on the end and not obstacles
- Put first things first
- Always think win- win
- Communication is the key
- Synergize
- Sharpen the saw

Chapter 12

25 Useful and practical tips for frugal living

INTRODUCTION

Thank you for taking your precious time to download and read my sweet handbook about *FRUGAL LIVING*. I am very confident that the material you will find here in will shower you with valuable advice on how to manage your finances well so that you can build wealth and achieve your so much desired financial freedom.

Frugal living is essentially not a new concept as such but it has been becoming more and more popular today as people look for a way to get around the rather tough economical times. My main aim of writing this handbook is not just to highlight 1001 ways of how you can live frugally but rather, to cultivate the mindset of frugal living so that you can start thinking frugal and everything else will start from there.

I personally believe that we are what we are due to what we do and how we think. By having the courage to change some few aspects of your life, I know that you can give your life a makeover and start living abundantly. With most families today living from pay check to pay check, it is needless to say that having the right guidelines on how to realize your life's dreams, particularly on the financial aspect is something you seriously need.

The good thing is that with the financial advice highlighted here in, you will succeed in changing your financial outlook and start living a life full of gratefulness and abundance. Here in, you will find proven strategies, steps and tips on how to live and enjoy a frugal lifestyle that will in the end enable you to take full control of your money and achieve financial freedom.

Regardless of the financial situation you are in currently, this handbook will empower you and show you the right path towards realizing your financial goals. I will give you strategies and steps that you can adopt to ensure that debt doesn't burden you anymore. With the kind of financial freedom that you will achieve, you will be able to enjoy a good life that will keep your family and yourself happy forever.

I sincerely hope that you will find reading this handbook very enjoyable but the most important thing is to put the advice I give you into immediate practice. You will realize that frugal living is more or less an old fashioned lifestyle but what you need to understand is that it is an approach that will assist you to live a more fulfilling life.

You will realize that as far as frugal living is concerned, there are some few basic rules that you will need to follow. If you stick to the guidelines I have highlighted herein, you will be able to create a strong financial foundation for your family with no negative impact on the quality of life that you would wish your loved ones at home to have. Read on and know how you can live a good life full of happiness on a budget.

CHAPTER 1

WHAT IS FRUGAL LIVING?

So, you have finally decided that you now want to give frugal living a shot? Welcome to the club that will show you exactly how you need to manage your finances and build wealth. Of course you are wondering what is expected from you. Does frugal living mean that you doom yourself in a life where deprivation is the order of the day just for you to save a couple of cents?

Not at all! The truth of the matter is that living frugally isn't about living a life of deprivation and sacrifice. The whole idea behind frugal living is living smarter which will enable you live the kind of life you have always wanted to live. In fact, frugal living is more than just a lifestyle as it is indeed a state of mind.

As a human being, you can aim to generate a lot of income but without smart spending habits, you won't be able to build your wealth and achieve financial freedom. Frugality is a concept that helps you manage your money wisely by stopping those money leaks while at the same time being able to live a fulfilling life. To succeed in this, a mindset adjustment is required. After all is said and done, you will come to the conclusion of the fact that frugal living is indeed worthy it.

Frugal living is in itself a very broad concept and to ensure that you get a better understanding of all that is expected of you, here are a couple of things that will help you.

FRUGAL LIVING MEANS WISE MONEY MANAGEMENT

By knowing the amount of money you have and how much you need for covering your monthly bills, it is possible for you to spend your money wisely. Making better money spending and management decision isn't always that easy but it is crucial if you want to succeed while living frugally. For instance, you will be able to know if you afford buying a new shoe or not. Also, you will be able to know if that is the right time to purchase your dream car or not. The most important thing is to create a frugal budget that will guide your money spending behaviours.

With a good budget, you will be able to know what you are able to afford for now but most importantly, you will be able to know that you can't afford. In addition, this will also give you an idea on exactly where you stand when it comes to your saving goals, debt repayment and investments. Managing your money smartly is the first step towards taking charge and control of your finances and making your money work for you.

FRUGAL LIVING MEANS SMART SPENDING

Smart spending means taking the money that you have now and stretching it as much as possible. Also, it means that you focus more on getting the best deals possible on each and everything you buy- yard sales, shopping thrift stores, barter boards, clearance racks and auction sites. By doing this, you will be able to get what you want to buy at the most affordable price.

Actually, this is a very important part of frugal living because how you spend your money has a direct impact on your ability to build wealth and will consequently make or destroy your efforts of achieving financial freedom. Spending smartly mean that you even go to the extent of using rebates and coupons and combining them with sales in order to get the best prices possible on your groceries. Frugal living means that you even go to the extent of stockpiling those items which you are able to find at unbeatable prices.

Most importantly, frugal living also means that you know when it is not the right time to shop regardless of how urgently you need that item. If a purchase isn't fitting in your budget, you should hold it off for the time being until you find the most appropriate time to buy it. It requires you to wait patiently for the item to come down to your affordable price.

Adopting the habits of shopping frugally will help you a lot to control your spending. In the end, controlled spending means that you will have more savings to build wealth and even before you know it, you will have achieved your financial freedom.

FRUGAL LIVING MEANS BEING CREATIVE

Harnessing your power of creativity forms the center stage of frugal living. What this means is that you find ways that can help you make due with just what you have and learn doing more for yourself. For instance, you can change your oil by yourself rather than paying a mechanic to do for you. Rather than buying a new pair of jeans, frugal living means that you sew a patch on the hole. Also, re-use plastic grocery bags instead of buying trash bags and with such creativity, you will be amazed at how much money you can save and start building your wealth with day.

Every day comes with its new opportunities of creating, reusing and repurposing. As a frugal person, you need to be very alert and able to recognize such opportunities as they emerge and seize them right away. Before long, you will be able to turn such incredible opportunities into savings and you will definitely be on your path towards financial freedom.

As you can see, it is becoming clear that living frugally means that you rethink your spending habits, correct those habitual money spending and management habits which hurt your financial welfare and come up with ways of taming your expenditures and getting more out of what you have. More often than not, people's views of being broke every end month is due to mental choices which dictate their financial life.

In addition to this, failure to understand your own actions and habits as well as cash flow cycle is a major factor that contributes to your financial troubles. If you want to live frugally, you will want to educate yourself well on how you get and spend your money. This calls for you to take the initiative of right sizing your spending habits and monetary actions in a way that complements your existing financial circumstance and focusing to save more.

Frugal living technically means putting your financials in order by reducing your spending or spending smartly and managing your money wisely so that you can have more savings that you can use to build your wealth with. For you to succeed in this, it is of paramount importance that you become comfortable with how you manage your money and extending what you have as much as possible without creating scarcity.

The fundamental aspect of frugal living is that you will need to commit yourself to a planned based way of spending. In this regard, you will need to shift your spending habits and focus more not only on buying what you must buy for now but finding the best deals possible on what you are buying.

Frugal living means that you explore all the alternatives available that can help you get the most bangs for your coin. For instance, if you buy your shoes at the mall, you might want to explore alternative options so that you can buy the shoes at lower prices. Online stores for example are the best place to get great deals and offers on shoes and buying your shoes from these stores definitely means better deals and more savings.

However, frugal living is more than simply spending your money wisely and making some savings in the end. This is because you can only build wealth by managing the money you save wisely and knowing the right investment opportunities that have better returns that can make you build wealth fast but sustainably. From a comprehensive perspective of frugal living, you must also be able to manage your pleasure expenses and debts, investments and your savings properly.

By the end of the day, frugal living will help you take full control of your financial work. The strategies you adopt should aim at making your money work for you rather than against you. Once you are on the right path of making wealth, frugal living will help ensure that you keep on building your wealth without turning back. In the long run, you will be able to achieve your financial freedom and live a better quality life with your family.

In conclusion, frugal living is both a lifestyle and a mindset and understanding this is very important when it comes to ensuring that you are able to live the kind of life which you have always wished to live. This can only be achieved if you live smartly and ensuring that you get the best value for the money that you already have.

CHAPTER 2

WHY LIVE FRUGALLY?

So, we have come to the conclusion that frugal living revolves around better money management, wise spending, creativity and bargain shopping. But exactly what does living frugally add up to. Is it possible to have a better life through frugal living? Absolutely!

Living frugally can unlock a world of endless possibilities and enable you to reach to new financial heights which you have never imagined before. With frugal living, you will be amazed at how you can be able to pay all your debts off, fund your children's education, travel around the world and still enjoy the security that comes with having a fat account at the bank.

It is possible to make all these become a reality with frugal living. This kind of lifestyle will help you determine how you want your life to be and find a way in which you can make it happen. By saving a few dollars here and there, this won't lead you to a life full of deprivation but rather, a life full of endless possibilities.

But exactly why should you live frugally and why is it that financial expert usually recommend people trapped in debts and financial troubles to start living frugally? Well, to start with, living frugally allows you to spend much less than what you earn. You can then use the difference for paying off your debts, investing or saving. This is of paramount importance because you can only achieve financial stability by living a cheaper lifestyle than what you earn.

Secondly, you will realize that the less money you spend in your life, the less money that you will need to earn. What this translates to is that you can opt to work less and enjoy a more fulfilling life or work more still but still retire early which is equally awesome. Another alternative that frugal living gives you is taking mini retirements. As you can see, frugal living gives you more options than you can probably imagine.

You may even have more specific reasons why you need to live a frugal lifestyle. For example, you could be saving to buy a new car or taking your family to that big vacation. In such a case, frugal living will help you minimize your spending and manage your money wisely so that you can save more to buy what you want.

In such a case, you could be living a frugal lifestyle with short term objectives which is in still good. Nevertheless, it might even be a good idea that you continue living this good lifestyle even after you have accomplished what you want to do since it will help you build wealth sustainably and enjoy financial freedom thereafter.

Through frugal living you can be able to succeed in rejecting consumerism and be able to erase those unnecessary expenses and spending from your life. When economic times get tough, everyone might need to make some sacrifices so that they can direct their financial life to the right direction. Or maybe you would be better off spending your hard earned money on certain things that add more value to your life. Whichever ever way you look at it, frugal living will help bring sense into your financial life.

Living frugally is something you should consider if you want to succeed in making some budget cuts that will help ensure that more money stays in your pocket.

CHAPTER 3

HOW TO BREAK YOUR BAD SPENDING HABITS

Bad spending habits are among the top reasons why you might find it quite difficult to live a frugal lifestyle. Unfortunately, most people today have a tendency of spending their hard earned money frivolously. You for instance come out of your local grocery store with a cart full of things that you don't actually need but you simply bought them since they were being sold and you thought you might need them. Also, maybe it is that you can't avoid the temptation to buy need books despite the fact that you have a great library near you where you can get all the reading materials that you want.

If you are in the habit of spending money unnecessarily and you are trying to live frugally, you will find that your bad habit is seriously becoming detrimental to the financial goals you have set for yourself. To ensure that you are in full control of how you spend your money, here are a couple of things you can do and achieve your frugal living goals.

USE CASH ALWAYS

Use of credit card to buy items can make you spend more than you initially planned to. So, to control your poor spending behavior, discipline yourself to use cash at all times when you are going to the mall and ensure that you buy only what your cash permits you to buy. Once you have spent all the cash you have, go home. This will particularly help you stop struggling with paying off credit card balance which could be hindering you from accumulating wealth and achieving your financial goals.

MAKING A SHOPPING LIST ALWAYS

When you are heading out to buy office supplies, groceries or some materials for your upcoming DIY project, make a shopping list that includes exactly what you want. Avoid going into the store only with a vague idea of what to buy in your head. If you do so, you will find yourself spending a fortune on buying those 'bargains' that you even don't need. By the end of the day, most of these purchases will only be cluttering your home and you will have used your money for apparently no justifiable reason. Going to shop without this list can also make you forget some vital things as well and spend your money on less important items.

HAVE SOME 'SPEND-NOTHING' DAYS

One of the most powerful ways in which you can be able to break your bad spending habit is by having days in which you spend nothing. In fact, you can challenge yourself to spend nothing for an entire weekend. Even when going out, leave your credit card and cash at home and you will find that you will be able to control your spending behavior greatly. Also, this is also a time in which you will be able to explore exactly what you can do out there for free without having to spend even a penny out of your pocket.

MAINTAIN A SPENDING LOG

Write down what you spend for a period of two weeks. Your spending log should record the time, what you bought, the place and finally, how much you bought the item for. By doing so, you will be able to have an idea of where you are spending most of your money and tame unnecessary expenditures that could be frustrating your efforts of achieving your financial goals. You should expect some nasty surprises in the log such as those occasional treats and coffees which could be a daily indulgence for you.

AVOID CERTAIN WEBSITES AND STORES

Every one of us has those particular stores, be it online ones or on high street which you could be tempted to buy. In case you are sure that it is hard for you to browse without making a purchase, you should avoid such stores completely. Make sure that you burn yourself from such a website or store for a certain amount of time and you will be able to bring your spending behavior into control. If you are attracted to certain online stores, you can even take the step of blocking them in your browser and avoid the temptation that comes with mindless shopping at such stores.

CHAPTER 4

HOW TO DEVELOP A GOOD MONTHLY SPENDING PLAN

As highlighted here above, one of the fundamental aspects of frugal living is controlling your spending. By developing your monthly spending plan, you will be able to live and maintain a frugal lifestyle, save more money that you can direct to various investment opportunities to build your wealth. Here is a step by step guide on how to go about it:

TOTAL YOUR EARNINGS

The first step in developing your monthly spending plan is to know how much money you will earn in the morning. In this regard, calculate the amount of money that you will get after taxes this month. It is important that you include only income sources which you are completely sure that are dependable and that you will actually earn the money.

MAKE AN ASSESSMENT OF YOUR MONTHLY EXPENSES

In this step, make a list that details your regular expenses per month. This should include the amount of money that you plan to spend on having fun such as entertainment, hobbies or eating out and even the minimum payments which you intend to make towards settling your debts. Have a rounded figure of your intended monthly expenses.

GET THE DIFFERENCE BETWEEN YOUR EARNINGS AND MONTHLY EXPENSES

The figure that results after you make the subtraction shows the amount of money that you will be left with after the regular monthly expenses are covered. This will give you an idea of the remaining money that you should expect to have after meeting your monthly expenses.

SUBTRACT OTHER EXTRA EXPENSES

Do a quick review of your spending plans for the month and note any other extra expenses which you will likely incur. This is because all months of the year are not always the same and while some of the months will involve relatively low expenses, others will have extra expenses which you should account for in your spending plan as well. Such could include expenses such as scheduled home or car repairs, dental or medical bulls, trips, parties, subscription renewals, extra meals out and even holiday related purchases. You should subtract these extra expenses from your figure in step 3.

CREATE A CUSHION

Once your anticipated expenses are all covered, the next thing you should do is to check at the amount of money you still have left. Then, you should be able to determine if the amount of money is that is left can adequately cushion you against the unexpected expenses, i.e. medical bills, home or car repairs and even missed work time. It may happen that you might not know how much extra you should build in but according to experts, 10% is always the rule of thumb and you certainly can never go wrong with it.

REWORK YOUR BUDGET

Chances are high that your budget might turn out to the negative side and in such a case; you should go over your expenses again. This time, look for various places in which you can make cuts by starting to cut down your spending on the items that you feel you can afford to do without or you can do with less of it. You should keep reworking your budget over and over until it finally works to your satisfaction.

INVEST IN YOURSELF

Once you have determined the amount of money that has remained, use the cash to start paying down your debts. Alternatively, you can decide to channel the money towards building your investments and savings. Know how much money you will invest and most importantly, review your investment opportunities carefully. It is essential that you avoid investing in high risk ventures because even though they might have a high return, you risk losing your hard earned money at the same time. In this regard, know the kind of risk that you can afford to should and make well informed investment decisions.

Making a good monthly spending plan is something that you should take very seriously as it is the gateway towards building your wealth and achieving your financial living. Frugal lifestyle requires that you keep your monthly spending at its minimal and in this regard, you should be able to find areas where you can make cuts and ensure that your spending is at its lowest.

Also, to ensure that you have adequate planning time, it is essential that you make your monthly spending plan well before the month starts. This will ensure that you have sufficient time to play with your spending and know the kind of expenses that you will be incurring when the new month sets in.

Also, keep in mind the fact that your spending plan is bound to change based on the changing circumstances. As such, it is important that you are not afraid to make the changes as it deems necessary. It is however very important that you are watchful of the kind of changes that you are making and ensure that they are not against your frugal lifestyle. Make only the necessary changes which you have no option than to make otherwise try as much as possible to stick to your original plan.

It is also worth noting that there are no two months which are exactly alike and you should thus expect some differences from one month to another. In fact, you should ensure that you make a new monthly spending plan for each month just to ensure that you are making decisions based on your most current spending. However, to make it much easier for you to create your spending plan, you can make the necessary adjustments to your previous monthly spending plan. This is because some costs such as rent, fuel expenses, meals etc. are bound to remain the same regardless of the month in question.

When you are trying to achieve the frugal goals you have set for yourself, having a budget that is well planned will really help you a lot. As such, it is important that you consider making such a budget so that it can guide you accordingly as to how you can manage your finances and be a step closer to achieving your financial freedom.

CHAPTER 5

PUTTING YOUR SPENDING PLAN TO WORK

Once you have finalized making your monthly spending plan or a frugal budget for that matter, the next step is putting it to work. First, you will need to check and confirm that your budget covers all the monthly expenses you expect to incur and your financial goals. Now, you need to test it and check out how it actually feels. At first, you might find it a little challenging trying to adapt to a frugal lifestyle but you will need to do your best to live within the limits of the budget that you have set for yourself.

Assess your budget and see if it is leading you towards achieving your set financial goals. At end month, spend some time to have a look at your expenditures and see if they are indeed matching up to the budget that you have set for yourself. In case they aren't, you will need to determine a good action plan that will help you stick to the spending plan that you have created. Sometimes, you might need to actually rework on your budget so that it can reflect how you are actually spending your money.

Keep assessing your frugal budget and making the necessary adjustments over time until it conforms to your lifestyle and until it is in life with your financial goals. In fact, one thing that you will need to keep in mind is that you can never finish making a frugal budget. You will need to continue looking over and over the budget each and every month so that you can be able to catch the areas where you could be possibly overspending. Keep on crunching on the numbers again and again until you get it right finally.

When creating a frugal budget or a spending plan, it is very important that you are very honest with yourself when it comes to your spending habits. This is because doing so is the only way you can be sure that you will be able to have a budget that is more realistic. Also, most people forget budgeting for fun which is a mistake that you shouldn't make. Actually, budgeting is not total deprivation. Remember that you should also make some budgetary changes as you go on and you should certainly not be afraid of making such changes.

A good frugal budget is highly evolving in that you will need to keep on adjusting it from time to time so that it can be near perfection. Having copies of your bills with you will help you a lot in coming up with a more realistic budget as you will be using more realistic figures.

CHAPTER 6

HOW TO ELIMINATE YOUR PERSONAL DEBT

When you are trying to set aside some money for the future, you might find that your personal debt is always draining you down. Finding yourself stuck knee deep into debts is one of the things that can frustrate your efforts of achieving your financial goals. In such a case, building wealth becomes nearly impossible as every penny that enters in your pocket ends up coming out through the other pocket to pay the interest.

If you find your debts level rising instead of not dropping, you should know that everything is not alright and you should do something to tame your finances. You might even find yourself contemplating to borrow some more money to use for paying off the interest that your current debt is making. In such a case, you might see as if there is no end in eliminating your debts and your financial welfare could only be getting worse and worse with time. To help you manage your money prudently and somehow reduce the debt, here are a couple of things that you should consider doing:

USE COMMON SENSE

Most people find themselves buried deep in debts for not using their common sense. In fact, the main reason why most people are always complaining of debts is due to the ease of obtaining and using credit. Most people never realize the amount of money they have spent already and before they even come to their senses, they find that they have maximized their credit cards out on monthly basis. If you want to have an idea of the amount of money that you are spending, it is good that you pay in cash for everything. Use your credit cards only for emergency purposes like for medical emergencies and those unexpected car expenses. If you pay in cash, you will be able to appreciate every single dollar that you earn.

AVOID IMPULSE BUYING

The only way you can succeed in freezing your debt is by freezing your spending particularly if you lack a high income for supporting high debt levels. However, if you find yourself incurring more and more debts, you are going to find yourself unable to have enough funds for paying off the interest. So, to keep things short and simple, don't make impulse purchases unless you are dealing with an emergency.

DEVELOP A GOOD PLAN

Financial experts always insist that failing to plan is planning to fail and this piece of advice actually applies to every person on individual level and family households alike. Take some time to develop a good road plan which is going to lead you to that much desired debt free zone. The first thing you will need to do is to know the amount of total debt that you have and know how long you will need to pay off the debt considering your current debt payment plan. Then, establish a budget that will help you cut back on those unnecessary expenses so that you can have more funds available for paying off your debt.

RESEARCH ON VARIOUS OPTIONS THAT WILL HELP YOU SAVE MONEY

There are many money saving opportunities such as credit card offers and low interest rates that will help you get out of your debts fast. For instance, before you settle down on a certain creditor, make a point of shopping around so that you can get the best deals. The good thing is that most creditors nowadays are very eager to negotiate their rates and you can take advantage of this to see how you can reduce your debt.

TAKE ACTION

After formulating a plan on how you will save money, get into action right away and follow your plan to the letter. A good debt management strategy will help you reduce your debt gradually, step by step but you also need to have the will power of doing so. Discipline is of paramount importance if at all you are going to set yourself free from the chains of debts and live debt free.

CHAPTER 7

PSYCHOLOGY OF FRUGAL LIVING: ARE YOU READY?

With economic reports predicting even tougher times in the future, the importance of starting to live frugally now cannot be underestimated in anyway. If you are wise, it is a high time that you tighten your belt and start to learn what frugal living is all about as it will truly save you. But before you even start considering the benefits of frugal living, the main question that you should be asking yourself is whether you are ready psychologically for this kind of lifestyle or not.

Living a frugal life is in itself not an easy affair as such and you will need to be psychologically prepared for it. The main question that you should be really asking yourself is whether you are ready for the new lifestyle or not. To succeed, you must be willing to commit yourself to a life of a new kind of life. It is not always as easy as such to change lifestyle but by working through certain psychological issues, you will be able to really go quite a long way in ensuring that you are successful.

The first and most important priority that you should have is getting rational and defining your goals. For instance, are you aiming at trimming your budget by a certain amount or do you need to revamp your lifestyle completely? Also, do you have a certain amount set up in your mind that you intend to save? Rational thinking really helps a lot and it is in fact much more important than emotional thinking. There are various factors that you must consider such as a catastrophic reduction in the insurance fund you have set or sudden unemployment.

You need to be firm and committed to your goals as this will give you a sense of being in full control over the plans you have and increasing your likelihood of being successful. Something else that you must also not overlook as you are in the process of defining your goals and objectives is the specific time frame of your lifestyle change. For instance, are you readying yourself for a reduction in income since you know you have only two years left since you retire? If your boss has forced you into early retirement the following month, you should ready yourself to make some sudden radical changes.

It is much easier to accept long slow changes from the psychological aspect than it would for sudden radical changes. By knowing this, you should be able to make your changes now instead of waiting until a catastrophe happens since it is easier to make small changes into new habits. Also, it is essential that you also overcome those pre- conceived notions that you could have. The main reason why most people end up being stalled is because they have no idea of what frugal living actually means.

Actually speaking, there are certain ways in which you can start living frugally even without having to feel miserable as such. Being frugal doesn't mean that you become cheap and miserly as there are other better ways of doing so. Think of frugal living as trying to be more economical or if you want less wasteful. This way, you will find it incredibly easier for you to adopt a new frugal lifestyle. A frugal life is less difficult compared to what you could be imagining. By planning carefully and discarding any pre-conceived ideas that you might have, you will find it incredibly easier for you to live frugally.

Once you have appreciated the benefits of living frugally, the most important thing for you to do is to have a game plan on how you can make this kind of lifestyle a reality. While the whole idea might not be very difficult, it is important that you have a certain goal in mind which you want to accomplish. By limiting how you spend, you are able to start reaping the benefits of a frugal life. Also, your whole family must work together still otherwise you will find it incredibly difficult if you try accomplishing all these on your own.

You will need to adjust your thinking and prepare you mind so that you can start living frugally. As you make a decision on whether you need to buy something or not, it is important that you ask yourself if spending the money on something else much better is a better idea for you or not. Keep in mind the fact that the whole idea behind living frugally is spending your money smartly and not spending. Once you have your priorities send, you will find that everything else will definitely fall in place.

You need to know the best kind of living conditions that you need and the kind of scarifies that you should make. This is very important because when it comes to living frugally, you will find that making sacrifices is the order of the day. In addition, living frugally doesn't mean that you deny yourself the opportunity of being happy and cutting off any kind of recreation from your schedule. However, you need to ensure that you include budget in your schedule as this will help you a lot in the long run to get your financial situation in control.

If you are a family person, it is also important that you train your kids to also start living frugally as this is certainly not a one person's affair. Let your children understand the fact that even though you can afford most things, you opt not to in order to save the funds for something better such as a big family vacation. Living frugally is substantially easier when the whole family works together. Living frugally also requires that you make a lot of personal decisions especially on how you will be spending your money and it is important that you don't go wrong about it.

CHAPTER 8

EMERGENCY FUND AND ITS IMPORTANCE

Even after you have succeeded in creating an awesome frugal budget, there are many other unexpected things in life which can be a stumbling block when it comes to achieving your financial goals. Even when you think that you are in full control of your financial boat, there are many other things that can frustrate your efforts and the worst thing is that these are things which you might not even have an idea that they will befall on you.

Having an emergency fund is something of paramount importance as this fund will really help you a lot in times of job loss, sickness, car repairs, home repairs and other unexpected expenses which are not reflected in your frugal budget. So in short, you must be well prepared to handle such things and having an emergency fun will eliminate the worries from you.

Here is how you can go about creating an emergency fund:

DECIDE THE AMOUNT OF MONEY YOU WOULD LIKE TO SAVE

Here, you will find yourself bombarded with lots of options ranging from a mere $1000 to a year's wages or more. It is essential that you have a good idea about the amount of money that you plan your emergency fund to have and you are the only person in a good position to determine this. In this regard, you will need to ask yourself the amount of money that will make you feel secure and save the amount in an emergency fund. In case an emergency expense strikes such as sickness, you can always get the financial aid from your emergency find.

DETERMINE YOUR MONTHLY EXPENSES

Calculating your monthly expenses become very important if you choose an amount based on several moths of your living expenses. Start by making a list showing your monthly expenses such as food, housing costs, debt repayments, utilities, insurance, transportation costs and much more. In short, this includes the must pay bills and once you have it in order, total the monthly expenses up and then multiply your resulting figure with your chosen number of months. For instance, if you have decided that you will be covering $2000 for three months in monthly expenses, this will require that your emergency fund has $7500 in savings.

OPEN AN ACCOUNT

After determining how much money your emergency fund should have, the next thing you need to do is deciding where you are going to be keeping your money. The most important thing is ensuring that your emergency fund remains fairly accessible. The last thing you want is to find yourself with an emergency expense only to find that you are not able to access the funds for one reason or the other. The best thing to do is to open an account which could be a money market account, short term deposit certificates or a savings account all of which make good sense. Having such an account ensures that you have the liquidity you want and the good thing is that your money will also be earning interest as well as it sits in the bank.

KNOW HOW MUCH MONEY YOU CAN SAVE COMFORTABLY

For the average person out there, building an emergency fund is something that tends to take some time and might even take you a lot of time. The most important thing is to be patient as this is very much okay. Once you start saving, don't stop but keep on saving little by little and before long, you will be able to have accumulated a lot of money. Have a good look at your finances so that you can determine the amount of money that you can afford to save to the emergency fund every month. Even saving just $10 per month is going to help a lot in the long run and you have no reason to worry whatsoever if you are sure that is the much you can save.

SETTING UP AUTOMATIC DEPOSITS WILL HELP A LOT

You can even make saving much easier for you if you schedule automatic deposits for your emergency fund. By doing so, you just need to sit back and see your balance continue to grow month after month and be assured of financial security.

FIND ALTERNATIVE WAYS OF BOOSTING YOUR SAVINGS

One of the pillars of frugal living is creativity whereby you come up with different ways of boosting your savings efforts to help your emergency fund grow even much faster. This will help you reach your set savings goals much faster and if you are really serious about it, you will be amazed at how things will work out to your advantage.

10 REASONS YOU SHOULD HAVE AN EMERGENCY FUND

The modern day society is one that encourages spending and more spending and it becomes much difficult for people to appreciate the true power of savings. Your emergency fund serves the same job as a savings account and will really help you achieve the goals of your frugal lifestyle. If something unexpected arises, the emergency fund protects other long term investments that you could be having. By using the money available in your emergency, you are assured of not withdrawing from your retirement account which may lead you into paying penalty taxes.

Also, with an emergency fund, the last thing you need to worry about is to have to sell off your long term investments when emergency expenses come striking. Besides, having cash makes you want to buy nearly everything that come a long your way provided the owner has an interest of selling it. An emergency fund will motivate you to keep on saving little by little until a time when you will finally become financially secure.

Here are top 10 reasons why having an emergency fund is something you should take very seriously:

1. In case you lose your job, the emergency fund protects your family.
2. Provides a reserve for family emergencies such as health

3. Makes you able to pursue highly attractive investment opportunities which comes a long your way.
4. Helps you negotiate much lower prices when making major purchases.
5. Helps you avoid tax penalties as you don't have to use your retirement savings too early.
6. Saves you from losing money as you don't have to sell your investments during times of down markets.
7. Helps reduce stress which in turn increase well being and health
8. Helps eliminate most of the marital arguments.
9. Keeps you in a position of bargain purchasing other people's expense, i.e. others who need cash desperately
10. Creates a financial cushion that you can use for major car or household repairs.

CHAPTER 9

TIPS ON HOW TO ADAPT TO A FRUGAL LIFESTYLE

When you are trying to adapt to a frugal life, you will find lots of advices out there and you might even end up being confused. This is because you can go from something simple like turning the lights off at daytime to even grinding flour at your home to minimize on your spending. Considering all the different aspects involved in frugal living, you will be able to know too well that adapting to this kind of lifestyle is not always as easy as such.

Essentially speaking, how frugal you become will mainly depend on your lifestyle. To be regarded frugal might be as simple as thinking twice before buying something. Simply tiring the heat down at night will help you make some incredible savings on your utility bill and this certainly qualifies you to be regarded frugal. Shopping less is yet something else that you can do as well by thinking well on whether you need what you are planning to buy before actually ordering it.

Being frugal isn't really about re-using your ziplock baggies or even collecting rainwater or grinding your wheat at home. It is not even about the trip that you didn't go since you that that it was a sheer waste of your finances. It is all about thinking first before you spend. In fact, it is all about ensure that you conserve what you have and use it prudently. The hold idea is about increasing your savings and adopting good financial management habits.

Also, remember that when it comes to households, there are no two households that can ever be the same. All of us have different goals even though we could all be claiming to live frugally. One family buying a pickup truck for $50000 might not look frugal for some people. However, if we are in the business of hauling the cattle to the market for sale, then you know too well that it really becomes a necessity. There are many other ways in which you can make up for it. For instance, such a family can buy cattle feed in wholesale so that they can save money. Alternatively, they could take very good care of what they have, no matter how small it might be to ensure that it ends up lasting longer.

The main point in all this is that each household must be able to look at its own situation so that they can make sound decisions on exactly what they need so that they can become more frugal. Living frugally doesn't actually mean that you do without something and it even doesn't mean that you live a life without what you need. Rather it means just the opposite of this. You will need to be very careful when shopping as this is where you are bound to spend a lot. This not only means taking good care of your hard earned money but doing everything possible so that you can get the most out of it.

To succeed in your frugal lifestyle, you will need to spend much of your time making wise decisions that will pay off in the future. You should learn how you can make your hard earned money to work for you rather than against you and you should focus more on having more for as little money as possible. Living frugally means that you reduce what you are spending and live within your means. You should be able to take good care of all your belongings and this even includes your money as well. It is all about making well though goals and working towards reaching them. Rather than deciding where and how you will spend your money before you even make it, you should have good money management skills and know exactly where each and every coin of yours go. In this case, take time to carefully evaluate your spending habits. In fact, you might be surprised to note that how you spend your money is something of much more importance than even your income.

For instance, you could be making $50000 per month but if you find yourself spending about $75000 per month, then you can be sure that you are in deep trouble. Debt will eventually manage to catch up with you and this will seriously devastate your financial life. The whole point especially when it comes to spending is that you spend less money than what you actually make and this is the whole essence of frugal living. It is learning to live with what you actually have and not what you expect to have. Spending less is much easier than making more. So, in this regard, it is wise to say that being frugal is much easier than juggling lenders and credit cards.

After knowing how to manage your money smartly, spend less and save more, the next most important thing is continuing the process day in day out. The key to being successful while living frugally is spending less and saving more. Before long, you will realize that these concepts are going to change your life greatly and you will be able to ensure that your money is indeed working for you. You will need to learn how to become different from norm and start living smart.

There are so many things involved when it comes to living frugally and as you will find out, you can't manage to fulfill everything all at once. The most important thing is that you start slowly and work without looking back and before long, you will realize that everything will turn out alright for you. If you overspend in a certain area of your life, you can be sure that it is going to cost you in another area. Avoid living a luxurious life as this will only compromise your efforts to save. Living simpler is key to adapting to a frugal lifestyle and living your life to the fullest.

CHAPTER 10

FRUGAL LIVING IDEAS FOR HAPPY RETIREMENT

Of all the many frugal living ideas that exist out there, the most precious ones are the ones which help people retire. With the state of the economy continuing to be scaring, there are some people who feel that they are not ready to retire…at least not so fast and not now. However, there are some great frugal living ideas that will help you retire happy. This mainly includes those retirement options which cost less money.

Preparing for retirement is something that even the wealth persons know that it is something that can't be taken lightly. Regardless of how old you are, it is important that you start readying yourself for retirement. Unfortunately, this is one of those things in life which usually falls to the bottom most part of most people's priority list. However, being prepared, both emotionally and financially could make a big difference on how well you will live when your retirement years come calling.

One of the things that you should do so that you can be prepared for your retirement is maximizing your retirement saving plan out. There are some employers who even match contributions made by their employees to assist them retire gracefully. After adopting a frugal lifestyle, it is important that you speak to an expert so that you can understand the different retirement saving plans available out there and know the ones that suit you best. Don't make the mistake of reviewing the plans before finally settling down on the one that suits you best.

Something else that you should do as you get ready to retire is creating a 'Plan B' as this is something that you will really need. The 'Plan B' will essentially work as your back up plan which aims at ensuring that you still have an income just in case various factors like massive currency devaluation or stock market crashes deplete your retirement savings. In such a case, you should be thinking of an alternative way of making some income that you will be living on upon retiring. Such could be online marketing, consulting work or writing.

Something else that will help you prepare for retirement as you live frugally is by downsizing. Having a small house, less commitments and fewer possession is something that will help you make the most out of your retirement years. This is because when it comes to retirement, less is more. For instance, by having a small home, this also means that your costs for water, heat and air will also be low as well and this will help you make considerable savings in turn. This also means that you will spend less money to maintain your home and you will have more to spare for hobbies and doing things that makes you happy.

Creating a budget is something that you should take very seriously as you prepare for retirement. In fact budgeting is a very great idea that everyone should take very seriously at any given time. Frugal living while in retirement doesn't really mean cheap but rather being thoughtful especially on your spending. Living frugally essentially means that you find ways to economize and cut back. It essentially means that you seek out lower cost alternatives which surprisingly could be the best for your retirement especially during retirement. For instance, by not eating out so much and opting to cook food at home, this will not only help you save big but will also ensure that you eat healthily. Another way to live frugally is opting to repair things around your home instead of buying new ones.

It is essential that you focus on retirement options that cost you much less as this will mean that you will in turn be spending much less. This includes:

i. The RV retirement lifestyle: This is one of the best ways to retire and ensure that you are spending much less. In this regard, you will need to examine all costs that are associated with owning a home and replace them with the expenses you would incur if you are living in an RV. If you do the comparison, you will end up realizing that living on the road is a much cheaper lifestyle. For example, the monthly rate of being ain a good RV park may cost you about $500 and this even includes the utilities not to mention the kind of fun associated with RVing.

ii. Park model living offers a much cheaper alternative compared to the traditional home. Have you ever asked yourself where you could find a fully furnished house for just $15000? Well, you know that this is only possible at a park model community. Joining this frugal and fun way of life doesn't require you to have a lawnmower or a snow blower. You will just be paying a total monthly cost for park utilities and rental for just $500 per month or even less.

iii. Retiring overseas: This is yet another incredible option available for those who want to live frugally that most people unfortunately don't seem to keep into consideration. Places such as Panama, Ecuador and Mexico are known for having awesomely low housing costs and utilities that will only cost you between $500 and $750 in a month or less. The cost of health insurance in such countries is considerably low and you even don't need to keep asking yourself why most Canadian and US retirees opt to live in such countries.

So, if you are looking forward to your retirement any time soon, these frugal living ideas will help you enjoy a frugal retirement. Nowadays, retiring is supposed to be the happiest time in your life and you should welcome your sunset years with your two arms and not lamenting in anyway. Just pick the most ideal one for your retirement and start enjoying right away.

CHAPTER 11

7 IMPORTANT FRUGAL HABITS YOU SHOULD DEVELOP

No one else in the world is responsible for what really happens to you and your life but you. You can decide to keep complaining about things in life that you don't like or you can come up with a game plan to change them. Most importantly, this is directly related to your financial state. If you want to have full control of your life, you must start living frugally and you will no longer have to live from pay-check to pay-check.

Here are 7 key habits that you should develop if you want to start living a more frugal and happier lifestyle that will help you take full control of your current money situation.

BE PROACTIVE

First, you must take full responsibility of your life if you really want to succeed and you can only do so by being proactive. Regardless of your past, you can decide to decide how your behaviour will be now. By being proactive, this means that you should understand that you are in full control of day to day interactions that take place in your life. This will in turn determine the direction your life will take as well. Being proactive is the opposite of being reactive whereby you are not swayed away by the environment and blaming the external factors for your behaviour. Be proactive today and take full control of your financial welfare and commit yourself to doing so.

FOCUS ON THE END AND NOT OBSTACLES

Living frugally is always associated with a lot of obstacles and if you just sit there and focus on these challenges, you will never be able to commit yourself to your newly found lifestyle. As such, you must start by visualizing what you want to achieve by living frugally and then working towards achieving it. Don't let external circumstances influence the direction your life takes but have a clear vision and work towards accomplishing it. To visualize frugality effectively, you will need to start by defining your goals and have a game plan on how you will get there.

PUT FIRST THINGS FIRST

Start by asking yourself about the things which you find to be of great worth and more valuable to you and by putting such things first, you will be able to organize and manage your time well around your priorities and make them a reality. This habit will more importantly help you a lot when it comes to making decisions about your spending as you will be able to know exactly what you must buy and what you can afford to do without. For most people, saying no is one of the hardest things in life but you will need to make your goals first priority if you want your frugal lifestyle to bear fruits for you. First, make sure that you recognize the effect of your finances and learn to just say no when you have spent your budged amount.

ALWAYS THINK WIN- WIN

It is so sad that since our childhood, we are always told that our self worth is based on comparisons to other people and competing with our peers. The only way that you can measure our success is by the number of people we have failed. However, having a win-win mind set makes it possible for you to see and appreciate the mutual benefits of all your interactions. Creating frugal situations that are win-win is not always easy but this is not to mean that it is impossible. You will need to particularly be in a position of differentiating between net worth and possessions. Know how to measure true wealth and this will help you live a more effective frugal lifestyle.

COMMUNICATION IS THE KEY

Communication forms the desire of being heart and understood by others and this is something that you will really need when living a frugal lifestyle. To communicate effectively, you need to understand first and you will be surprised at how listening could help you become effectively frugal. In this regard, you will need to understand that you are not the sole stakeholder of your life and also understand the needs and goals of others. By understanding those around you, it becomes much easier for you to practice your frugal lifestyle.

SYNERGIZE

One of the best ways to learn new skills especially on how to be frugal is though team work and interactions. Synergizing refers to the habit of cooperating creating and working as a team with others in order to solve existing problems in the best way possible. To succeed with your frugal lifestyle, it is important that you bring your personal expertise and experience to the table and know how you can achieve your frugal goals easily. To synergize effectively for frugality, you will need to look for new and better ways of doing things and surround yourself with frugal people. Having likeminded people in your vicinity will really help you achieve your goals since you share similar objectives.

SHARPEN THE SAW

When it comes to achieving the kind of lifestyle that you want, whether it is frugal or any other, remember that you are the greatest and most important asset. So, what this means is that you will need to take very good care of yourself, emotionally, physically, spiritually and mentally. Take some time to renew and rejuvenate yourself in such areas so that you can accomplish your goals. Remember that frugality doesn't imply that you give up all your luxuries and those things that contribute to your happiness.

Becoming a highly frugal person is a gradual process that you can't accomplish overnight but day by day. Living frugally is incredibly rewarding and provided you start out with the right attitude, you will be able to conquer all the challenges that you meet along the way. You learn day by day and make gradual adjustment to your lifestyle so that you can achieve your objectives. Take time to evaluate your life and see the different aspects that you can take advantage of to capitalize on your frugality.

CHAPTER 12

25 USEFUL AND PRACTICAL TIPS FOR FRUGAL LIVING

1. **Go with just one car:** most families today operate with at least two cars and they barely know how this negatively impacts on their financial welfare. It is a well known fact that after the house, the car is ideally the next most expensive item. Beside the initially high price of buying the car, car maintenance can also cost you a fortune and things could even be worse if you have several cars. So, frugal living requires that you stretch yourself as much as you can to manage with just one car and this will help you start taking charge of your financial life.

2. **Opt for a small car:** a smaller car will help you save thousands especially when it comes to fuel expenses. For instance choosing to drive a car rather than a SUV can help you save big on gas. While it is important that you be comfortable, overdoing it will only devastate your financial life.

3. **Live in a smaller house:** simply because you are in a positioning of affording a larger house does not give you the green light to live in one. Frugal living requires that you live in the smallest house that can make you feel comfortable. So, don't stock your family of five in a single room apartment as the point here is being realistic depending on your family size.

4. **Rent instead of owning**: This is something that has always attracted a lot of debate but don't blindly think that buying is a better investment. Owning a house comes with mortgage interests, maintenance and insurance costs which you can evade if you decided to rent. The best thing to do is to compare between renting and owning and make a sound decision.
5. **Stop online impulse buying:** shopping online is quite addictive especially because you do it with your credit and tend to think that it is not costing you. This is due to the ease and convenience that comes with online shopping and you can easily engage in impulse buying. Buying online is recommended as it helps you save money but you should buy only what you need.
6. **Try a minimalist wardrobe:** living frugally also means that you check on your wardrobe as well. Generally, you should be wearing casual pants or jeans, a polo- type shirt or T-shirt and sandals and you will be good to go. Having less clothes will save you a lot of time and will help reduce the budget that you spend on clothes significantly.
7. **Carry your lunch to work:** most people think that ordering pizzas and other convenience foods for lunch is stylish but have no idea of how this hurts their finances. If you can bring your lunch to work, the better for you if you want to start saving big.

8. **Eat out less:** if you have to eat out for one reason or the other, do it frugally and spend the least amount of money you possibly can. The average person has been found to spend at least $2000 per year by eating out. Fast foods can be very expensive not to mention the serious health hazards associated with eating some of these foods.
9. **Shop for used stuff:** buying used items can really help you save a lot of money even though you will be sacrificing the joy of having a brand new item. If you need to buy an item, start by asking your friends and they might direct you to a person who don't need or use it anymore. You can shop for used items at thrift shops and garage sales where you are assured of finding great bargains on the items you need.
10. **Avoid shopping:** The worst thing you can do is to go to a department store or shopping area and start shopping around without an idea of what you want to buy. By doing this, you will end up being tempted to buy stuff that you really don't want. Shopping for fun or as a kind of entertainment can cost you a lot in the end.
11. **Commute by bike:** commuting by bike isn't a display of poorness but it is something that comes with a wide range of advantages. Besides saving you gas which is the main objective of frugal living, using the bike to go to work or school will help you stay physically fit while at the same time helping you stay physically fit through exercising.

12. **Ride the bus:** if biking isn't your cup of coffee, why not consider riding the bus to work. Public transportation offers an awesome way to save money but unfortunately, this is something that many people ignore without knowing how it can help them make big savings.
13. **Walk:** most people often drive to a school or work place which is only a mile away from where they live. Walking is a great alternative to driving to your work place every morning as it will help you save gas and burn some calories as well.
14. **Frugal exercise:** it is important that you exercise your body to stay fit. However, this doesn't mean that you pay a fortune for your exercises as this will only succeed in devastating your financial welfare.
15. **Stay healthy:** by staying healthy in the first place, this will save you costly visits to the doctor's office and having to buy some costly medicine in the end. Prevention is always better than cure and eating healthily and exercising is simple and effective.
16. **Use the library:** buying books is something that we are always advised to do but this can be very expensive. Instead, it is better that you check them out at the library where you will find a large selection of books.
17. **You don't need cable:** This might not go down well with many people but the truth of the matter is that cutting out cable will save you lots of money every month. The other great thing about cutting out cable is

that it will help you do things such as going outside, having conversations and reading which you might not be able to do if you had cable at home. So, it is a win win situation by not having cable.

18. **De-clutter your home:** well, selling your clutter won't help you save money as such but when you are living frugally, it will help you have more money that you put to income generating activities and succeed in achieving your financial freedom.

19. **Quit smoking:** This might not be an easy way for many people to save but if you can, you will be able to really save big on those cigarettes which only succeed in making you unhealthy. Smoking also comes with high long term medical costs as well which further devastates your financial life as well.

20. **Drink alcohol in moderation:** drinking a couple of beer bottles adds up to a significantly high amount of money in the long run. The bottom line about alcohol drinking is that it is very expensive and only frustrates your efforts of achieving financial freedom.

21. **Free entertainment:** look for cheap ways for having fun and avoid entertainment options that cost you a lot of money such as buying concessions or going to the movies.

22. **Frugal gifting:** gifts may end up costing you quite a significantly lots of money and it is important that you know how you can give gifts frugally. Give consumables

as they are cheap or make a gift yourself rather than buying one.

23. **Learn to stay at home:** It is true that staying at home might sound boring but you should know that being at home enables you to stay in a peaceful and quiet environment away from the troubles of the world. This is also the time to bond with your family and loved ones and in the end, you will be able to save big in shopping expenses, eating out and gas.

24. **Cancel those subscriptions:** given the vast amount of information available on the internet, is it sensible for you to still subscribe to those magazines? Must you also subscribe to a newspaper with all those news online? The thing with subscriptions is that they just succeed in helping you spend significantly more on things you can find easily and cheaply online.

25. **Travel frugally:** Finally, travelling can be one of the most expensive engagements you can ever do. Travelling frugally includes considering travelling by train as it is cheap, shopping around for cheap car rentals, flights and hotel rooms. Also, only travel when it is a must and reduce your holiday vacations to just one in a year or none at all until you are financially stable.

www.ingramcontent.com/pod-product-compliance
Lightning Source LLC
Chambersburg PA
CBHW051820170526

45167CB00005B/2098